The Sunderland Echo

IMAGES OF
WEARSIDE

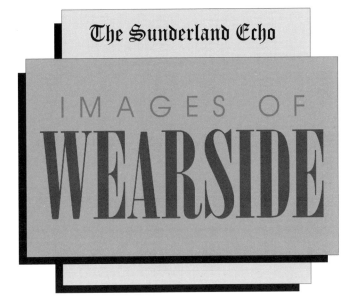

Researched and written by
Maurice Boyle

The
Breedon Books
Publishing Company

Published by
The Breedon Books Publishing Company
Breedon House,
44 Friar Gate, Derby, DE1 1DA

ISBN 1 873626 78 9

Jackets printed by BDC Printing Services Limited of Derby.
Printed and bound by Hillman Printers, Frome, Somerset.

Contents

The Old Town Hall which gave Sunderland's main street its dignity and a focal point. It was designed by Brightwen Binyon in the 1880s and its clock tower and chimes were much loved by the townspeople. Its entrance steps were a favourite place for people to meet at in town. For many years athletes tried to run the length of Fawcett Street while the clock struck midnight, but it was never accomplished. The greatly-admired building, opened in 1890, was demolished in 1971 much to the dismay of many Wearsiders.

Introduction

WEARSIDE'S known history goes back to the seventh century, but this book concerns itself with much more recent times . . .times within living memory and those that have fallen within the gaze of the nineteenth-century invention, the camera.

The Sunderland Echo has long been aware of the passion Wearsiders have for nostalgia. Several years ago the newspaper published a series of booklets, *Canny Aad Sunlun*, and *Wearside at War*, the popularity of which confirmed the yearning Wearsiders have for reflecting on the past.

The *Echo* is in a unique position to present a pictorial record of change on Wearside. From Whitburn in the north, west through the Boldons, Washington, Chester-le-Street, Durham City, and south to the sea below Peterlee and Easington the *Echo* has kept watch on a large part of the region for more than 120 years.

The photographs in this book have been taken from our archives that go back to the early part of the century. They have been supplemented by generous lending on the part of *Echo* readers who have responded to our appeal for contributions for the book. The latter response has allowed the inclusion of many unpublished photographs that give a fascinating insight into life in the good old, bad old days.

However, the 300-plus pictures published represent less than one per cent of those in the *Echo* archives and therefore this collection is but a snapshot of the huge subject that makes up a century of life on Wearside. The emphasis is not necessarily on the most important or significant events that took place on and around Wearside. That in itself would take many volumes. Rather it sets out simply to provide a flavour of the times.

We believe that a useful purpose is served by recording those times in pictorial fashion so that our heritage is not left to wither and be lost. The contents are loosely sectionalised for the convenience of the reader and some photographs might just as suitably have been included in other sections.

There was misery and hardship aplenty in the past. There were wars, disease, unemployment, injustice, class-consciousness, and grinding poverty to be endured. For today's older generations, it is all too easily recalled.

There were, however, compensations to balance the scales . . . neighbourliness, a sense of belonging, a clear knowledge of what was right and wrong, and an optimism and wealth of spirit that

Not until they can see Penshaw Monument from afar do County Durham folk consider themselves to be nearing home after they have been away. Built in 1844 by public subscription as a monument to John George Lambton, the Earl of Durham, it is twice the size of the Temple of Theseus upon which it is modelled. It is visible from many miles away as it sits atop Penshaw Hill. In recent years it has been floodlit and on its lofty site appears to be floating in the air at night.

enabled people to set aside their troubles and let their grit and good humour light their way. For the young there was the wonder of innocence.

Such values are held in lesser regard today, not because they are invalid, but rather because modern life has left them behind in the pursuit of materialism and hedonism. We would like to believe that this book may cause people to pause and consider whether those values again might play a greater role in the fabric of life.

So it is that today's older generations look back affectionately to the Hot Potato Man providing a miniature feast for queues outside the Royal Cinema in Bedford Street, Sunderland. To remember what a treat it was to get a saveloy dip after a visit to High Street Baths. To savour again the smells and sounds of Jackie White's Market, and the luxury of Pompa's ice cream parlour down in High Street.

Recalled with affection, too, are the dances at the Rink and the Seaburn Hall. They sparked off thousands of Wearside romances, many of which led to the altar. In those days Roker Park Football Ground was hardly ever occupied by fewer than 50,000 spectators on match days. Pubs only sold real ale and a traffic jam on Wearside would have made headlines.

For the children there were days at the seaside, Sunday School train rides to Coxgreen, *Monday Night At Eight* on the wireless, hot home-made bread, sledging down the park banks, tram rides to town, and a 'school in the morning' cry from mam as she heralded bedtime.

Younger readers of the book will get a peep into the past from which they have come. They may giggle and laugh at the dress and the transport, but they have no option but to accept that they are simply the next model down the line and that they, in turn, will be replaced by another generation who may giggle at them.

We believe that the pictures in this book will rekindle memories and perhaps bring a smile, a sigh, or even a groan . . .there is no doubt that today's Fawcett Street in Sunderland has but a shadow of its former grandeur.

Images of Wearside is an attempt to evoke these feelings in young and old. It seeks to place on record how things were, warts and all, but, most of all, it offers you the reader the opportunity to take from it what you will

Let's take a walk into the past . . .

Maurice Boyle
Sunderland
March 1994.

Wearside ...
The Way It Looked

Fawcett Street, Sunderland, looking north very early in the century. The Town Hall, with its much-loved clock and familiar chimes, stood a proud sentinel in mid street. The new-fangled electric trams with their open tops and sparking overhead wires began a new era of public transport on Wearside.

Looking south in Fawcett Street, Sunderland, on a misty day in 1922. A single-deck tram is in mid view and a man can be seen on an extending platform doing street light maintenance.

A Circle tram approaches the Gas Office Corner of Fawcett Street before World War Two. 'The Shop at Binns' advertisement on public transport had already become familiar. The extending platform for street lighting maintenance is again in operation on the extreme right.

It's 1953 and Fawcett Street retains its grandeur despite the bombing of the Binns stores. The trams are much more comfortable and they move passengers with speed and efficiency. The Economic bus on its way to its Park Lane terminus can be seen in the mid distance.

The junction of High Street West and Bridge Street in 1953. Two-way traffic, including trams and buses were beginning to cause jams as the number of private cars coming on to the roads began to soar. Walkers the jewellers on the west corner was a favourite shop for window-gazing.

Bridge Street, looking south towards Fawcett Street, believed to be in the 1940s. St Mary's RC Church afforded weather protection to people waiting for public transport with two convenient shelters. Lloyds furniture and radio store is offering cycles for two shillings per week and lawnmowers for one shilling weekly.

Right: The Town Hall steps and entrance, a favourite meeting place for generations of Wearsiders. Flanked by the attractive, ornate lamp standards it was also the scene of many civic ceremonies and announcements.

Below: A sight to bring a sigh of dismay to older Wearsiders . . .the demolition of the splendid old Town Hall site in 1971. Opened in 1890 it graced the town for more than 80 years and most Wearsiders lament its passing. "Fawcett Street has gone downhill ever since," is a familiar complaint.

The north end of Sunderland Station in 1933. The Circle tram stands at its terminus as cars pull out of Union Street. A sign over the canopy advertises a trip to the Middlesbrough versus Sunderland derby game for three shillings.

Inside the north end of the station was a buffet room, the Station Master's Office, and a Ladies' Room. There was also a wonderful machine, much beloved of children, that enabled one to punch one's name on to a tin strip. At the left of the entrance was the Bricklayer's Arms, more commonly called the Station Buffet.

Above: The south end of the station with its arched roof was just as busy as the north end though with fewer features. Finlays tobacconist's booth always did a roaring trade in those days of Willie Woodbines, Craven A, and Capstan cigarettes.

Right: An unusual view over the station from the bomb-damaged north end clock tower. It shows Union Street to the left with a Northern or S.D.O. double-deck bus passing in front of Joseph's travel and sports goods shop.

One of the finest buildings on Wearside houses Sunderland Museum and Library. It was opened in 1879 and its foundation stone laying in 1877 was attended by General Grant of the United States. Generations of Wearsiders have been entranced by the wonders they saw as children in the natural history gallery, not least Wallace the lion.

Another historic occasion on Wearside was the opening of the Police Station and courts in 1908. Civic dignitaries queue to go inside while ranks of policemen present arms to the rear and the band (right) take a breather.

The old cast-iron bridge over the Wear in 1883 when tolls were still in force. A train puffs across the railway bridge as ships and paddle tugs go about their business on the river. A lively drawing of the period.

The new replaces the old. This photograph taken around 1928 shows the new Wearmouth Bridge being built over the old one. Cranes and a box girder structure make a confusing picture, but tiny figures can be seen working at the very top of the bridge. A silver rivet was incorporated in the structure.

1929 and almost complete. Already the trams are running across Wearmouth Bridge and the box girder structure is being dismantled. Robert Thompson's Bridge Dockyard is in operation in the shadow of the railway bridge.

The Seaburn Hotel under construction in 1936. The top sign board advertises Tram-O-Car tours at two pence for a sea coast trip or one shilling for a town tour as far out as Grindon.

*The ornate frontage of the old **Sunderland Echo** Office in Bridge Street, with its 'Bridge Clock'. The picture boards in the front window always drew plenty of viewers, especially if they had had their photograph published in the **Echo**. The clock now graces the newspaper's headquarters, Echo House, at Pennywell.*

An early photograph of Monkwearmouth and Southwick Hospital. It was inaugurated in 1873, as the Monkwearmouth Dispensary.

A remarkable old photograph that vividly recaptures the mood of the times. The old East End Market at the foot of High Street was opened in 1830. This picture was taken in 1930 when times were very hard for the ordinary folk of Wearside

Fulwell children gather at the tram stop in Sea Road (then called Sea View Road) for the annual Sunday School treat between the wars. Girls in bonnets and boys in caps was the order of the day.

Not all that well known is the fact that the once familiar police box was invented on Wearside by Chief Constable Frederick Crawley. This one which stood in Kayll Road, Sunderland, is believed to have been the original.

The Central Reading Rooms and Junior Library was housed in a temporary one-storey building next to the Town Hall after bombing during the war. It was well used in a period when reading was one of life's main entertainments.

Still to be seen today but hidden away out of sight is this fine Italian marble on the side of the Three Crowns Hotel, in High Street West, Sunderland. Standing opposite the north end of the station, the pub was one of the biggest and busiest on Wearside. The building now houses a furniture store. Watson Moralee was the landlord during the war and into the mid fifties.

The age of steam is long gone but not forgotten on Wearside. The smells of steam, smoke, and hot oil must have come back vividly to those fortunate enough to see the famous Flying Scotsman locomotive come panting through Sunderland many years ago.

This photograph of the boys . . .and girls . . .of Sunderland Orphanage was taken around 1894. It shows the children in their sailor suits and hats with the master and his family at the rear.

St Peter's Church, Monkwearmouth, was founded as a monastery in ad 674 by Benedict Biscop. Around 680AD a boy of seven entered the monastery. He became The Venerable Bede, renowned throughout the world as a great Christian scholar.

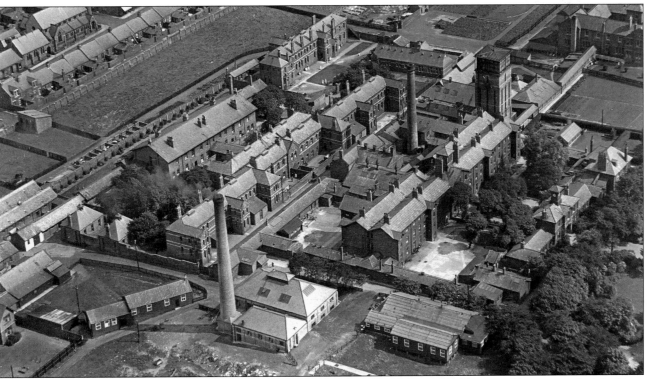

An aerial photograph taken in 1938 of Sunderland Municipal Hospital looking from above Hylton Road. A keen eye might spot nurses in their white uniforms in the area top centre.

The baker's and grocer's shops of W.H.Garbert in Pallion between the wars. Mrs W.Patterson, who lent the photograph, believes the errand boy to be a lad called Bob Alcock.

Another of Mrs Patterson's pictures shows Westmoor Cricket Club around 1926. They played on what are now Hylton Road Playing Fields.

Bowler hats and best coats for the foundation stone laying of Monkwearmouth Branch Library. Beards and moustaches were the rule, rather than the exception they are today.

Monkwearmouth Station, Sunderland, was designed by a Sunderland man, Thomas Moore, in 1848. It is a fine example of railway architecture and has drawn praise from many parts of the world for its pleasing lines. It now houses a splendid museum.

A familiar picture on Wearside, but worthy of repetition, the Hot Potato Man. With his little barrow-boiler he traded outside the Royal Cinema in Bedford Street, Sunderland, for many years. Scalding-hot potatoes with salt were a treat on a cold winter night while waiting for the tram or in the cinema queue.

A more leisurely time just after the war when sheep might be driven down John Street, Sunderland. It recalls even earlier days when sheep and cows were delivered live to butchers who then did their own slaughtering.

The Wheatsheaf junction, Sunderland in the 1940s. It was right for Roker, left for Southwick, and straight ahead for South Shields and Newcastle. The lighthouse corner is prominent and the Sunderland Corporation Transport HQ is on the right of the picture.

The Kings Cinema in Crowtree Road, Sunderland, was opened in 1906. It was destroyed by bombs during the war and stood as a ruin for many years before it was demolished. The advertisements on the corner are for Heinz tomato sauce and Bovril.

One of Sunderland's best-known stores was Liverpool House. This old photograph shows the premises at the corner of Nile Street and High Street. Judging by the motor car it was taken between the wars.

Caslaw Bros Ltd was established in 1928 in premises at the corner of Bedford Street and High Street West. The business served the merchant navy uniform and bespoke menswear trades and expanded in mid century. However by the 1980s trade was beginning to fall off and the long recession of the early 1990s saw the business close. Mr David M.Caslaw lent the picture.

West Park Central School in 1948. Most of these boys will be in their 60s, says Mr George Prince, who is third from the right in the back row. The form master is Mr Leslie Potts who died within the past year.

Newcastle Road, Sunderland, in 1935. Wilson's Sawmills can just been seen on the right. The road was later widened to improve traffic flow. Photograph lent by Mr George Prince.

Five little girls from James William Street School, Sunderland, entertain soldiers from World War One. The lender, Mr George Prince, says his mother is the girl second from the right.

A hospital, a school, and now part of Sunderland University, this building has filled several roles since its completion in 1823. Perhaps it is most fondly remembered as St Mary's School when its yard would resound to the clamour of playing children.

The junction of Southwick and Newcastle roads had Sutton's smithy and the Cora Cinema which opened its doors in 1907. It was one of the town's smallest cinemas and it finally closed in 1959.

Grangetown, Sunderland, in the early 1950s. An old Guy single-deck bus is on its way to Dawdon and Marshall the chemist advertises the then new National Health Service.

The Palatine Hotel (now the Mowbray Park Hotel) at the junction of Borough Road and Toward Road was a popular meeting place for Wearsiders. This picture dates from the 1920s.

Wesley Hall in Trindon Street was one of many places of worship on Wearside that have disappeared and passed into history. It was renowned for its lusty hymn singing.

Right: Sunderland Parish Church, Holy Trinity, in the East End was built in 1719. Splendid, but sadly neglected, it was in recent years chosen as the city's finest existing building. Sunderland's first Council Chamber and library can still be seen there. Holy Trinity was the first brick-built parish church in the country.

Below: Thousands of Wearsiders learned the three R's at 'Jimmy Willies' . . . James William Street School, one of Sunderland's oldest and best-loved places of learning. It was the town's first Board School and could accommodate 1,000 pupils.

The distinctive tower of St George's United Reformed Church at the junction of Belvedere Road and Stockton Road is a familiar part of the Sunderland landscape.

The Grand Hotel in Bridge Street, Sunderland. Here visiting dignitaries and stars appearing at the Sunderland Empire would stay. For many years it was the leading hotel on Wearside and its restaurant was the place to be seen.

Standing in a prominent position at Southwick is the well-proportioned Holy Trinity Church (1842), focal point of the community and today an oasis in a busy world.

Crowtree Road in the 1950s. In the centre of the picture is Louis ice cream bar. Here children were taken for a treat and the young generation did their flirting and parading. Bergs cycle and radio shop and Tates electricals shops also stood in the same block.

High Street Baths entrance. Thousands of Wearsiders learned to swim at these baths with their immodest changing cubicles and chilling waters. The baths have now gone but the entrance has been tastefully incorporated into a nearby building.

Belford House once the residence of the Thompson shipbuilding family was given over as a recreational facility for shipyard workers. Its popularity remains undiminished.

Situated in the heart of Sunderland is the church of St Michael and All Angels, Bishopwearmouth. It has medieval origins and has been much rebuilt, most recently in the 1930s.

Jackie White's Market is part of the folklore of Wearside. This picture, if the mini skirts are anything to go by, must have been taken in the early 1970s.

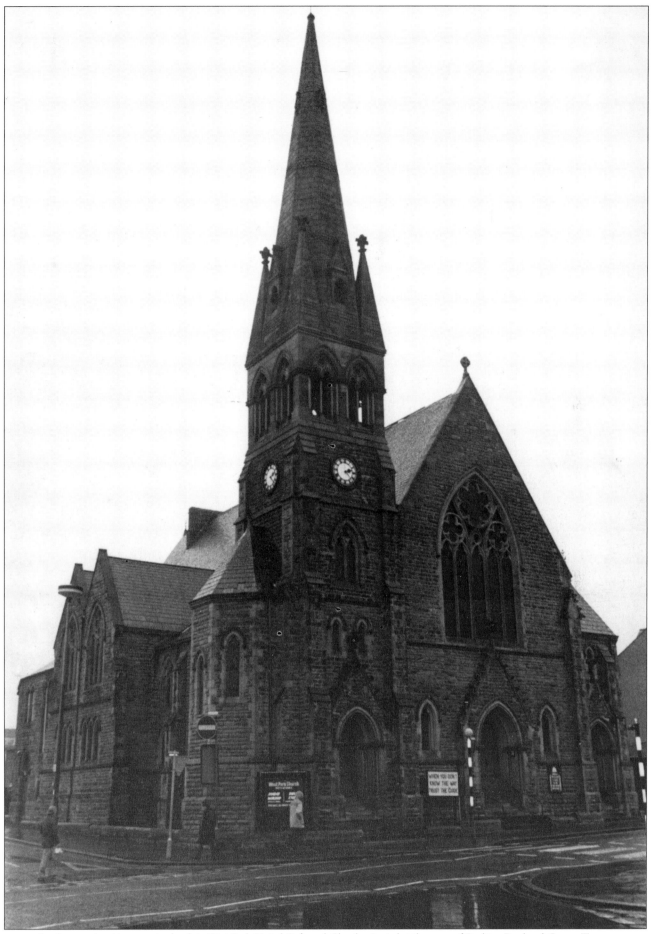

Another prominent town centre church is West Park United Reformed Church, situated at the corner of Stockton Road and Cowan Terrace.

Above: This cannon dates back to the 1640s and was dredged from the Wear. It has stood in Barnes Park for the best part of a century and has been a source of wonder for generations of children.

Right: Bodlewell Lane, Sunderland, viewed from the ferry with Low Street to the right. The tiny white spot on the pavement at the rear is the spout of the old Bodlewell pump. The photograph was taken in 1937. The name probably derives from 'bodle', an old coin worth about one-sixth of a penny, perhaps the cost of drawing water from the well.

Bede School was once the town's leading education establishment. Its fine buildings on Durham Road, opened in 1929, have had many pupils through its doors who went on to distinguish themselves worldwide in various fields of endeavour.

Above: The magnificent Winter Gardens at the rear of the Museum were popular all the year round. This pre-war picture was taken on a fine day with Wearsiders enjoying the sun on the terrace.

Right: A familiar sight down in the East End of Sunderland in the early part of the century are these women in shawls that were so much a part of the dress of those days.

Another of Sunderland's red-brick schools, Barnes School, in Mount Road. During the war it was damaged by bombs and its pupils enjoyed an unscheduled holiday for many weeks.

The Wesleyan Chapel in Sans Street, Sunderland, was known as Sans Street Mission. Built in 1793 and enlarged in 1807 it could accommodate about 2,000 people. This photograph was taken in 1937.

This photograph, taken before World War Two, is of the old police courts in West Wear Street which also housed the office of the weights and measures inspectors.

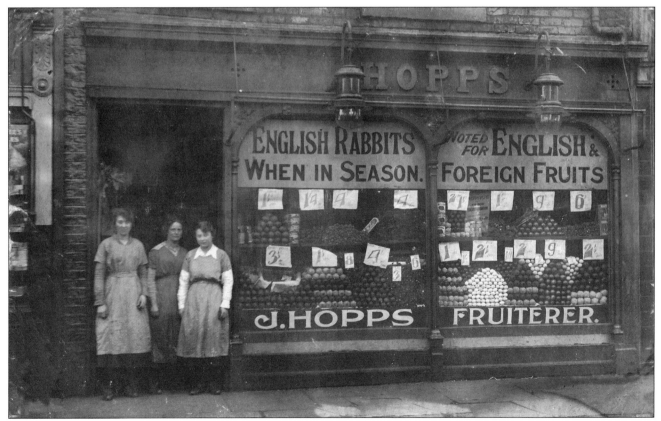

There were several Hopps fruit shops in Sunderland and this one is believed to be that in Suffolk Street. Mr Charles Percy Lamb, who lent the photograph, says the woman in the centre was his aunt, Annie Lamb.

47

An unidentified wedding party of 1922 has been lent by G.Williamson. It shows the fashions of those days when people set out to make themselves look their very best.

Almost without exception these ten-year-old boys of Diamond Hall School, Millfield, wear those ties with collared jumpers so typical of the pre-war period.

Above: It's 1935 and King George and Queen Mary have been on the throne for 25 years, so these children at South Hylton are given jubilee mugs and chocolate in celebration. Nevertheless, one little boy doesn't look all that pleased.

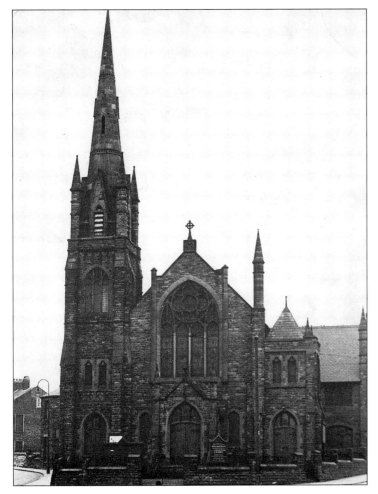

Left: Another fine building that disappeared to make way for road improvement was Durham Road Methodist Church which stood at the junction of Durham Road and Tunstall Road, Sunderland.

Above street level in Fawcett Street are some architectural gems. This ornately decorated terracotta frontage was designed by Wearside architect Frank Caws in the 1890s. Below was the very up-market Mengs Restaurant and function suite.

Another architectural masterpiece created by Frank Caws has been restored at the corner of Fawcett Street and High Street West. It is the Elephant Tea House of 1877. The nickname came from the elephants seen in the pitched-roof boxes on the top of the building.

It was the talk of the town when a tram overturned after colliding with a dray in Hylton Road in 1933. Thirteen people were taken to hospital but no one was seriously hurt.

Above: It is a mystery how this bus came to be hanging over an embankment in Newcastle Road, Sunderland. It is a Sunderland District Omnibus vehicle on the Sunderland-South Shields route and the date is believed to be just pre-war.

Right: Inside the Sunderland Technical College, students learned, among other things, the workings of marine engines. The college provided many of the Wear's shipyards and the nation's shipping lines with qualified engineers.

The Galen building of Sunderland Technical College in Green Terrace with its large clock and green dome. It does not look too different today in its role as part of Sunderland University, although the police box and the classic telephone box have long gone.

At the junction of Queen Alexandra Road and Tunstall Road there used to stand Strawberry Farm. The road in the foreground, still known as Strawberry Bank, leads up to Tunstall Hill the top of which affords the finest of views over Sunderland.

Another of the great spired churches of Sunderland is Christ Church which stands on Stockton Road. Built in the 1860s it served the people who were moving out into the then suburb of Ashbrooke.

After the war, the gap in Union Street left by the destroyed Empress Hotel, was used as a bus station for many years. There is little doubt that the bombing changed the face of Sunderland for ever.

The Durham Road-Seaburn via Fulwell tram approaches the Technical College as a Corporation bus passes over the railway bridge on its way towards Sunderland Royal Infirmary.

A Southwick-Grangetown tram waits at the Southwick terminus on a wet day on Wearside after the war. Nearby was the appropriately named Tramcar Inn.

King George VI died in February, 1952, and, as a mark of respect, all Wearside came to a halt for two minutes. Pictured are a tram driver and a motorist standing in silence at the south end of Wearmouth Bridge.

The Children's Hospital on Durham Road Bank. There can be few Wearside youngsters who did not pay at least one visit to the hospital during its many years' service to the community. It is now a special care centre for children.

Canal Farm, or Chapman's Farm as it was better known locally, at Ettrick Grove, Sunderland, in 1953. The prefabricated houses at Springwell can be seen in the background. The site is now part of the Barnes Park extensions.

One of the most famous views in the North-East is that of Durham Cathedral on its lofty site above the River Wear. This fairly recent photograph could have been taken 50 years ago for all the change that has taken place.

Left: Saddler Street, Durham City, in the 1960s with the Buffalo Head and Tucker's Cocktail Bar signs prominently displayed.

Below: The grim entrance to Durham Prison. One of Britain's oldest, it has housed some of the most notorious of the nation's criminals. Before the abolition of capital punishment its gallows sent many a murderer to meet his or her maker. It was here that the infamous child poisoner Mary Ann Cotton was hanged in 1873.

Brown's Boatyard on the Wear at Durham in 1954. A favourite leisure activity with local people, visitors, and the students at Durham University . . .an energetic row on the river. The oarsmen pictured here, however, appear to be in training for the city's annual regatta.

Durham City's distinctive bus station with its high glazed roof. It was a very busy station when this photograph was taken in 1952 with buses going to, from, or through almost every town and village in County Durham. The Sunderland bus always occupied the top platform.

At the height of the Great Depression of the 1930s the unemployed marched to Durham for a rally. In this early Thirties photograph the crowd is seen gathered in the Market Place. It takes a keen eye to spot a bare head.

The Sunderland to Durham bus pulls past the Belisha crossing beacons and into Belmont on the outskirts of Durham City in 1952. An Austin van and a Wolseley saloon car are the only other vehicles in sight in those days of quiet roads.

Taken between the wars this view of Church Street, Seaham, is a familiar one even today. But then every shop front was different and shopping for the housewife meant personal service every time. St John's Church is at the top of the street.

A forest of masts in Seaham Harbour in the days when steam was beginning to oust sail power at sea. A steam paddle tug and a few smoke stacks can be seen among wooden masts.

A day at the seaside has long been a treat for hardworking people. Here at the turn of the century the people of Seaham enjoy a summer's day in the traditional way.

Lord Byron's Walk has always been a favourite stroll at Seaham. Here it is pictured in its quieter days when its leafy beauty could be admired at leisure.

Seaham Harbour Cooperative Society in its early days. Almost every family joined and members never forgot their dividend number. There would be great excitement and treats when the 'divi' was due to be paid.

North Railway Street in Seaham Harbour with Young the printer and Clough the wholesale clothier prominently displaying their wares.

The old Deneside farmstead is surrounded by new house building as the Carr House Estate is constructed in 1936.

Seaham Hall one-time home of the Londonderry family and latterly Seaham Hall Hospital, stands in a green lawn site overlooking the sea just north of the harbour. The harbour, begun in 1828, shipped its first coal in 1831.

Castlereagh Road, in Seaham Harbour early in the century.

Carefree motoring days early in the century. These two open-top tourers are seen passing at the top of Houghton Cut. In those days cars got into bottom gear to climb the steep hill and woe betide you if you didn't have good brakes going down! The original 'Cut' was constructed by Napoleonic prisoners of war.

St Michael's and All Angels' Church, at Houghton-le-Spring, enjoys a lovely setting amid trees in the centre of town.

The White Lion Pub in Houghton-le-Spring in the 1960s before its modernisation. It was left for Newcastle and right for Sunderland at the junction where it stands.

The old brewery building in Houghton-le-Spring was in use until 1925 and stood empty for many years before becoming an entertainments centre in the 1970s. It became a night club but closed after a fire in 1992. A listed building, it still retains its charm.

Some of the first dual carriageway in the North-East is that of the approach to Houghton Cut. Here the construction work is under way in 1938. Note the big steam road roller in the centre of the picture and the Stoneygate pumping station in the background.

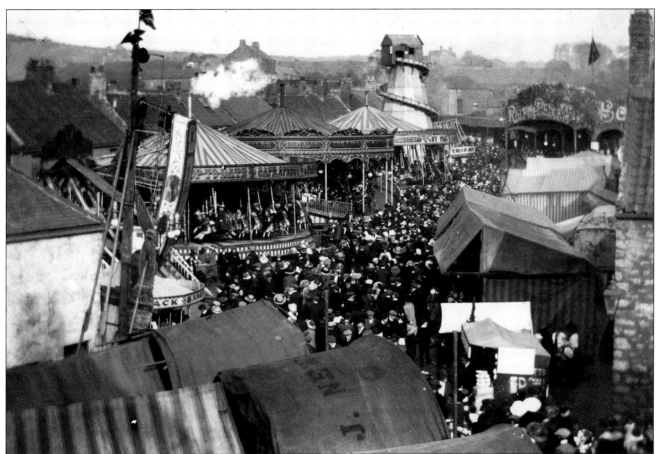

Houghton Feast still carries on but not on quite the same scale as it did in the 1930s when this picture was taken. A traditional helter-skelter can be seen in the background while to the left a giant shuggie boat is nearing the perpendicular. Traditional and undulating carousels are operating alongside each other.

Newbottle Street, Houghton-le-Spring in the 1920s. Traffic had not yet become a problem and a bicycle could be left against a gas lamppost without fear of theft.

Chester-le-Street a few years after World War Two. A steam train, leaving a plume of white vapour, can be seen crossing the viaduct on its way to Newcastle.

The new town of Peterlee quickly grew after World War Two. Six hundred years beforehand the Eden Hall farmhouse had its beginnings and became a building of great historic and architectural interest.

The southern end of Whitburn looks down to Roker Pier in this early twentieth-century painting.

Souter Point lighthouse just south of Marsden is best known on Wearside for its voice. The Big Grunter, as it was known, could be heard all over the region on foggy days. Now a National Trust property, visitors can view the light tower and keeper's cottage.

The Fishermen's Cottages at Whitburn between the wars. This row has long since disappeared and only a few remain today.

The lovely, ivy-covered front of Whitburn Hall with its life-size statues between the windows and its lush lawns which overlooked the cricket ground. The hall was demolished in 1980.

The old school at Ryhope. Taken before World War Two the picture shows excited children gathered round a delivery wagon to see what is going on.

The sturdy build of St Paul's Church at Ryhope stands out in this fine study.

A photographer was someone to be stared at in bygone days as these children in St Paul's Terrace, Ryhope, demonstrate in the year 1910.

Peace celebrations took place in Ryhope Street after World War One. Note the wooden downcomer and the bootscrapers outside the doors.

A composite picture shows the new for old slum clearance at Ryhope in 1937.

Davidson's Public House at New Silksworth became the Colliery Inn, and then the Drift Inn. This picture pre-dates World War One.

Silksworth Old Hall after World War Two looking across the lake to the croquet lawn.

Front Street South Hetton between the wars with kerb alignment work being carried out in mid picture.

Hetton-le-Hole between the wars when there was never a road marking to be seen.

Piper the butcher at Hetton-le-Hole with a delivery cart outside the shop.

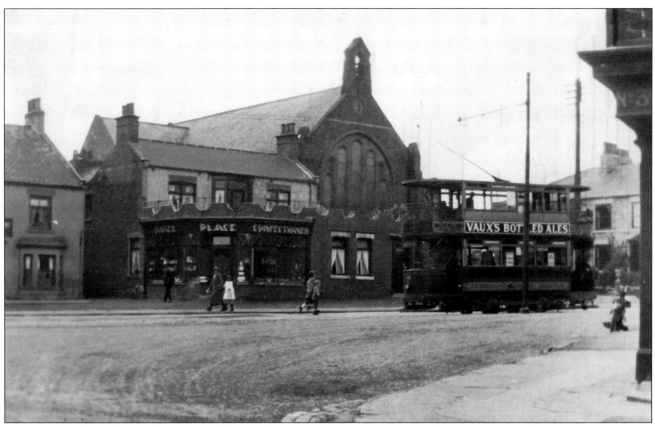

Sunderland District Tramways ran well beyond the borough's boundaries between the wars. This picture was taken in the Houghton-Hetton area.

Tram No. 15 at the St Aidan's stop in New Herrington, on its way to Houghton-le-Spring. The driver and conductor appear to be posing for the cameraman while the top-deck passenger and the pedestrians look on with interest. The picture has been lent by Mrs J. Cattermole.

An early century photograph of New Herrington lent by Mrs J.Cattermole.

A fine floodlit study of St Mary's Church at Easington.

79

Many collieries had their own bands in the Durham Coalfield and this was Easington Colliery Band taken in the 1930s. Sounding brass was a popular entertainment when every sizeable community had a bandstand for summer concerts.

The Hungry Thirties and the Miners' Welfare Hall at Easington was a busy place.

Easington Village retains its rural charm in this picture believed to have been taken in the 1950s.

Washington Chemical Works spoil heap dominates the landscape across the River Wear from Coxgreen in this picture from between the wars.

Another view of the Washington Chemical Works with a shunting engine (centre picture) tipping wagons.

The mobile preachers of the Church Army are featured with their wagon at Old Washington before World War Two.

Station Road, Washington early in the century. The North Eastern Railway houses are on the left and the second property on the right is the Post Office.

This part of Station Road, Washington, is now known as Barmston Close. The building on the right was formerly Washington Chemical Company offices.

Believed to have been taken at the turn of the century, this picture shows horse transport at the old Blackhall Rocks Hotel.

This old photograph shows the once familiar Elephant Rock at Blackhall.

The Palace Electric Cinema at Boldon entertained generations of Boldon citizens. Among the shows advertised is Joel McCrea in Gunsight Ridge *and Joan Crawford in the* Story of Esther Costello.

Glebe Farm at West Boldon on a lovely summer's day many years ago.

St Nicholas' Church, West Boldon, whose grey stones give way to brick for the crown of its steeple.

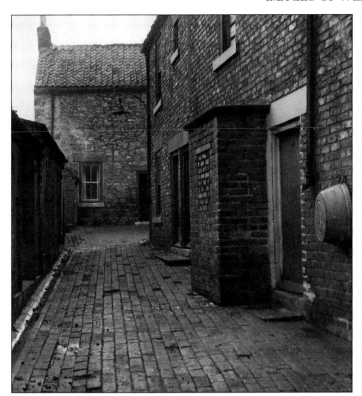

Left: A typical North Eastern backyard with a tin bath hanging outside and lavatories and coal houses across the yard. This is Binks Yard at Houghton-le-Spring between the wars. Right: An aerial view of the great pumping station at Ryhope. The smaller ponds were cooling devices for the huge boilers that drove the massive beam engine pump. The larger one is the reservoir.

Lowland Cottage at Boldon on the main Newcastle to Sunderland road is pictured in 1955.

The pump house at Ryhope was roofed over after the engine was constructed, so big was the machinery. The station went operational in 1870 and closed as recently as 1967. Steaming days are still held though no water is pumped.

At Work

No shipbuilding river was busier than the Wear in the 1950s. Cargo ships and tankers were turned out by the score and the tugs were kept busy servicing the big ships. This view looking west towards Wearmouth Bridge was taken in mid decade.

An old timer watches as another son of the Wear goes down the slipway and is taken under tow after launching.

The huge girth of the 45,000-ton bulk carrier Hupeh *can be seen as she leaves the slipway at the Deptford yard of Laings on the River Wear.*

Another busy scene on the Wear during the 1970s with tugs fussing around the newly-launched Ion.

Austin's Pontoon could lift medium-sized ships out of the water for repair. It was hardly ever idle and in its position just below Wearmouth Bridge its clattering riveters could be heard from the town centre.

Left: Shipbuilding involved many trades and here a grinding operation is in progress at Sunderland Shipbuilders. Right: This picture was taken from the roof of the old Echo building in 1941. It overlooks Austin's dry dock and shows a ship with a barrage balloon making its way downriver and past a camouflaged ship downstream.

Left: During World War Two women shipyard workers took over jobs vacated by men who went into the Armed forces. Here a group of women workers is seen painting a ship's hull. Right: It was not only unskilled work the women undertook during the war. Here two women get to grips with a heavy metal welding job in a Sunderland shipyard.

Left: Few people outside shipbuilding appreciate the size of ship's engines. As high as a three-storey house and a lot longer is a fair estimation of this monster in a Wearside engine works. Right: A very early century scene on the Wear with two paddle tugs moored at the quayside. A small boy looks on and perhaps forward to the day when he might work on the waterfront.

A scene to sadden many a Wearside heart as another nail is driven into the coffin of shipbuilding on Wearside. A huge crane is demolished at the North Sands yard a few years ago.

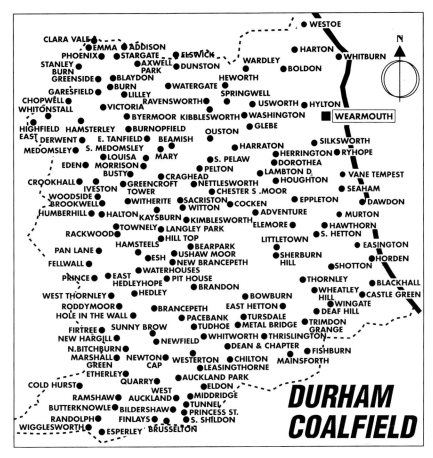

In the 1913 heyday of the Durham Coalfield there were 304 pits employing 165,000 miners. Today they have all closed. This map shows the coalfield as it was when the mines were nationalised in 1947, when there were still more than one hundred pits in operation.

Mining has always been a hard, dangerous job. This picture taken at a Durham colliery shows a shearer at work in cramped conditions.

Taking men and coal up and down the shaft is the job of the winding engineman whose communications telephone (foreground) to the pit bottom is a vital part of the operation. This picture goes back to the mid 1950s

Pit ponies go on exhibition many years ago at Horden. Note the shades over the eyes of the bigger ponies.

Far left: The miner's lamp. Perhaps the single most important piece of safety equipment developed for use in mines. It was developed by Sir Humphrey Davy and it prevented the ignition of gases by the lampflame.

Left: Wearmouth Colliery in Sunderland was the last to close, in 1993, but this picture goes back to the 1870s and shows the sinking of the third shaft at the colliery.

A strong bond is formed between pitmen and their ponies. These two are seen being pensioned off by their keeper many years ago after the last shift at the Adventure Colliery, near Hetton.

Mining has a turbulent history. This picture shows the police and miners in confrontation at Silksworth during the great eviction strike of 1891.

The miners of Silksworth were again in dispute in 1926 but so were all the nation's pitmen. This picture shows a group of Silksworth men showing support for the Daily Herald *newspaper, which championed their case.*

The miners of 1891 took to the roofs as the police and candymen (bailiffs) entered their homes and turned out their belongings into the street. The bailiffs had a key that would open every colliery house door. It was one of the bitterest industrial disputes in the coalfield.

In 1930-31 it was the Ryhope miners who were on strike. This picture is believed to show police escorting 'blackleg' labour to work at the pit.

Such was the incidence of accidents in mining that most collieries formed their own mines rescue teams. In times of need, help would come from all over the coalfield. This handsome vehicle with its quite splendid crew constituted the Houghton Mines' Rescue Team in the 1920s.

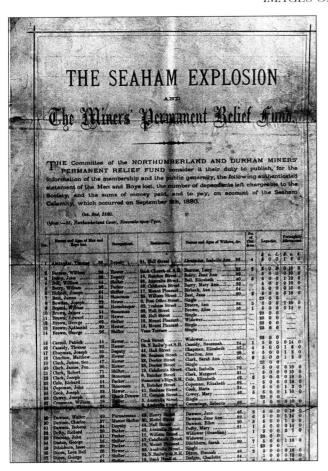

In 1880 a terrible explosion ripped through Seaham Colliery and 164 men and boys were killed. The youngest of them was 14. This poster lists the names and those of their dependants. It also lists the legacies the dependants received and the fortnightly allowances they were paid.

Scores of men and boys died in many other pit disasters, few more harrowing than the Easington Colliery explosion in 1951 when 81 men and two rescue workers lost their lives. The explosion occurred one and a half miles from the shaft bottom just as the fore shift was about to relieve the night shift. The scene depicted is of the dedication of a memorial to the disaster in 1954.

Whitburn Colliery in an aerial shot just after the last war.

The coal industry spawned others. Here at Hendon Gas Works in Sunderland 120 ovens turned coal into coke and gas. The contraptions on rails moved along the line of ovens and pushed the processed coke from the ovens for collection. The gas was extracted through the large diameter pipe.

Fishing on Wearside is as old as the port. Fish was a cheap alternative to meat in the days of depression when one could buy a basinful of herring for a few pence. Today the trade is much diminished and facing extraordinary difficulties. These men of a few decades ago enjoyed a more secure existence.

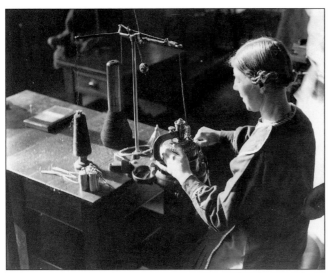

Left: It looks very complicated but it is simply a device for refooting stockings. The picture was taken just before the last war at the Blind Institute workshops in Sunderland Right: It is 1938 in the Nurses' Home in Murton Street, Sunderland. A typical wireless of the period sits on the mantlepiece while the nurses themselves appear to be keeping busy with knitting and reading.

Its a great time for the cats when a Sunderland fisherwoman in the East End gets cracking on a bit of filleting around the year 1935.

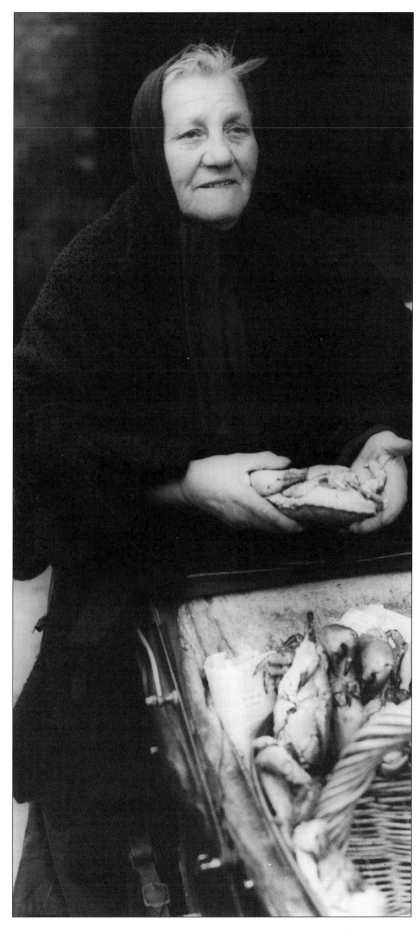

Left: Mrs Margaret Shipley was affectionately known as 'the Crab Woman'. She was a regular sight in the town selling crabs from a basket inside a pram. Freshly caught and boiled they provided many an appetising treat for generations of Wearsiders in mid century.

Right: Gypsy Mary' was a well-known character in Sunderland in the Thirties. With shawl and washing basket on her head she makes a striking figure.

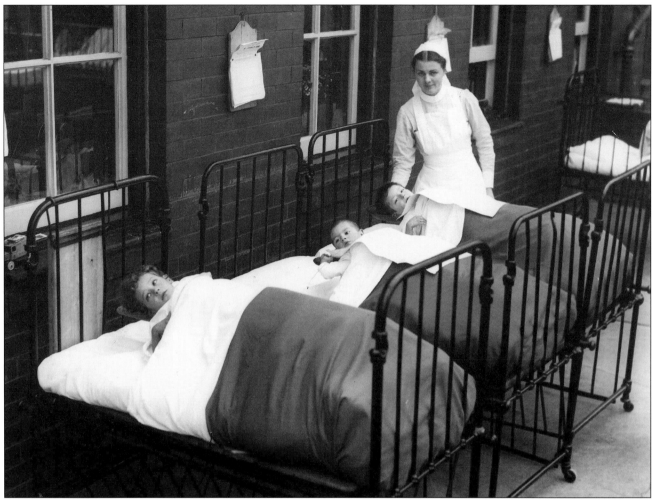

Child patients on the verandah of the Children's Hospital in Sunderland are attended by a nurse in pure white uniform and stiff collar.

A splendid photograph going back to the early part of the century shows a large group of men believed to be at the Londonderry engine works, Seaham.

After the War Ericssons factory at Pallion was a large employer of girls and women in the electronics industry. It later became Plessey Telecommunications Ltd.

An aerial view of West Pallion Trading Estate in the early 1960s with the Thorn Radio Valves and Tubes factory in the foreground. The factory produced black-and-white television tubes until 1974 when many people lost their jobs. It continued to produce colour tubes until 1989. The site has now been flattened and rebuilt. Mr Tom Purvis lent the pictures.

Loading tubes on to a conveyor at the Thorn factory at Pallion in 1962.

Nowhere was work carried out with greater intensity than on the river. Building, fitting out, repairing, and the busy coal trade meant that there was never a dull moment on the waterfront. This is believed to be an early post-war photograph.

The tugs were the workhorses of the Wear, pulling, pushing, nudging, and carrying. They made the river tick. The little fishing boats that scurried in and out of harbour to harvest the sea made sure that the river was always a busy place.

Left: A fine catch of cod awaits inspection by prospective buyers at the Fish Quay on the Wear before the last war. Right: Not many Wearsiders will recognise this structure. It is the Humbledon Reservoir which was originally open to the skies but which had a roof constructed about 50 years ago.

The friendly postman delivers a letter to one of the residents of Assembly Garth, Sunderland, just before the outbreak of World War Two.

Another resident of Assembly Garth takes delivery of milk from the milk boy. Note the jug, the churn, and the bell to alert potential customers.

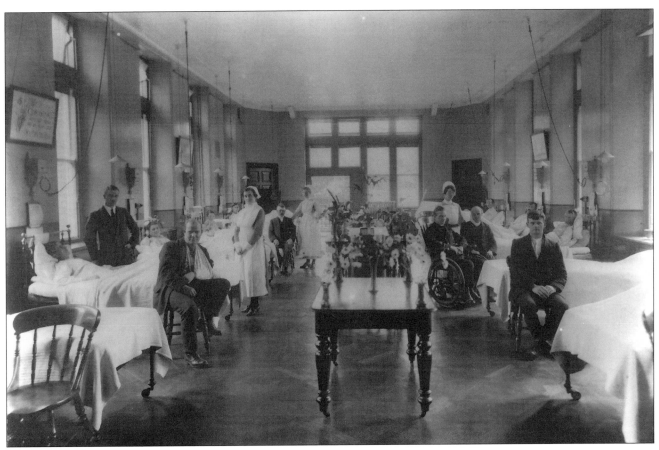

A fine series of pictures sent in by Mrs K.M.Marley show Sunderland Royal Infirmary at work in the 1930s. This one shows nurses with patients in a male ward.

The operating theatre at the Royal Infirmary. The surgeons bend over the patient with the anaesthetist at the patient's head. Nurses with sterilised instruments stand ready (right).

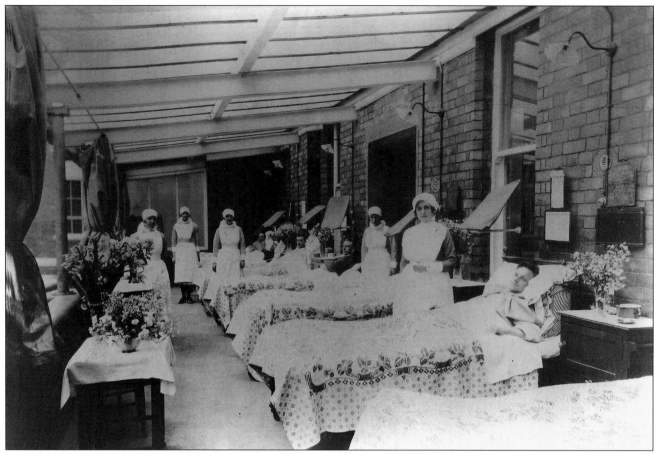

Out on the verandah at the Royal Infirmary usually meant that convalescence was progressing. The nurse to patient ratio here appears to be very favourable.

Above: Ford Paper Mill at South Hylton was a busy place when this picture was taken in 1966. More than 400 people lost their jobs when it closed in 1971.

Right: The Sunderland Echo has played a big part in the life of Wearside. Here in the 1930s the Dispatch Department crew tie-up bundles of the then broadsheet Echo ready for the delivery vans.

The distinctive black-and-green Echo *vans leave Bedford Square for all parts of town in the 1930s. A barrow takes* Echoes *to the station for further distribution.*

The Echo *composing room staff in 1943 pose beside their machinery. The compositors converted the raw copy into the lines and columns of type that make up the newspaper. They also composed the advertisements.*

The Echo *composing room in the early 1950s. The rows of Linotype machines in the background produced the type which was assembled in forms (frames) on the stone (benches) by the page make-up men in the foreground.*

Right: Selling newspapers has always been a tough job and in the nineteenth century it was tougher still. This statue of the Echo Boy was carved by Thomas Lackenby late in the 1890s. Three sculptures were made and one still can be seen in the Echo reception area at Pennywell, Sunderland.

Far right: A famous photograph showing King George V bending down to talk to a diminutive rivet heater-boy at Laings Shipyard during a wartime visit to Sunderland in 1917.

At Play

The Cat and Dog Steps sun-trap at Roker has long been a favourite spot for Wearsiders making the most of a fine summer day. If you look carefully you can see a man all dressed up in jacket and tie and wearing a trilby hat as he soaks up the sun!

Before the war the Holey Rock was another favourite sunspot for trippers. However the rock became unstable and in the interests of safety it was blasted away shortly after this picture was taken in 1935.

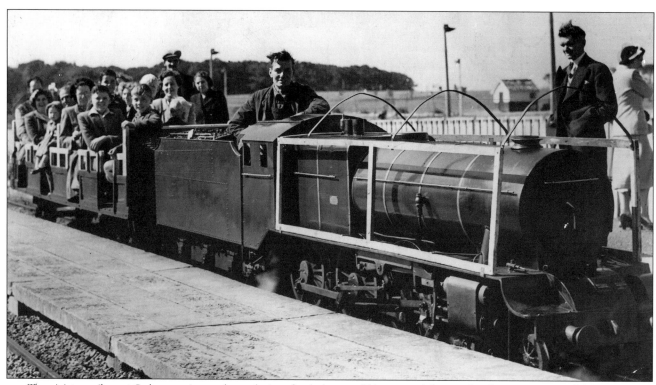

The miniature railway at Seaburn was immensely popular just after the last war. This was especially true when the carriages were pulled by a steam locomotive. Notice, too, that the passengers are not just children.

A trip to sea in a rowing boat was a great thrill for children as can be judged from their expressions. This picture was taken just days after the war in Europe ended and was lent by Linda Lowes.

A fine study of men contesting a tiddly-winks game on Wearside in the 1950s. Though not as popular or enduring as dominoes it called for great skill. The picture was lent by Linda Lowes.

From the dress it looks like the Roaring Twenties as this fashionable young lady enjoys a boat ride out to sea past Roker Pier.

Dodging the waves at Seaburn has been a daring pastime for generations of Wearsiders. This picture dates from pre-World War Two days.

The children's paddling pool at Roker after World War Two. Only a few inches deep, it provided endless fun for toddlers in complete safety.

This photograph of Seaburn was taken in 1929. The bus parked on the grass has come from Northumberland with a party of holidaymakers bound for the beach.

Roker Park looking out towards the seafront early this century. Walking through Roker Dene to the beach past the legendary cave called Spottie's Hole was a favourite stroll. Spottie was reputed to have been a smuggler.

Seaburn Fairground on a packed 1950s day. The Helter Skelter, the Dive Bomber, and the Big Wheel were guaranteed to provide squeals of delight while the miniature railway was always a favourite of the smaller children.

Opened in 1903 Roker Pier has protected the harbour for almost a century. In addition to that role it has given greater scope to sea-rod fishermen and provided a calm area of sea for budding yachtsmen.

Many a Wearsider did a spot of courting in the Seaburn Hall. All the big post-war bands played there at one time or another and many an aspiring singer took his or her first steps in show business on its stage. It was demolished in a seaside re-development programme.

Sunderland's first purpose-built cinema was the Villiers Electric Theatre in Villiers Street. It opened its doors in 1912 and showed its last film in 1958. Showing when this photograph was taken was James Stewart in It's a Wonderful Life.

Above: The Ritz was definitely at the posh end of the cinema scale. Standing on a prominent corner of Holmeside it opened in 1937 and it seated 1700. In its heyday queues formed hundreds of yards long to see such films as Mrs Miniver *and* Gone with the Wind. *The Ritz later was called the ABC and latterly Cannon.*

Left, top: Sunderland's biggest and most popular ballroom was the Rink in Park Lane. Formerly a roller skating rink, it had a huge dance floor that could take hundreds of dancers at a time. A balcony gave watchers a grand view of the dancers whirling below them.

Left, bottom: Some of the country's top bands played the Rink including Geraldo, Ted Heath, Edmundo Ros and Victor Sylvester. The Civic Ball and Press Ball were the highlights of the year. Alas the Rink is no more, having fallen to the developers.

A wet evening outside the Royal Cinema in Bedford Street in the early 1960s. Inside it was all plush seats and the wonderful songs and scenes of South Pacific *emanating from the screen.*

Above: Organ interludes were part of the cinema package. It was thought marvellous when the lights went up for the interval between films and up from the floor of the orchestra pit, blasting away with a rousing Sousa march would come the cinema organist. This organ, a Compton, graced the Blacks Regal Cinema in Holmeside, which later became the Odeon.

Above: Opened in 1882 the 3,000-seat Avenue Theatre stood in Gillbridge Avenue and can still be seen as part of the Vaux Breweries complex. Sir Henry Irving played the theatre which fell into decline as the bustling Empire Theatre went from strength to strength. The Avenue switched to films and prospered for a time but eventually closed with the advent of the talkies in 1932.

Below: A well-loved cinema the Havelock in Fawcett Street was special. Upstairs cinema-goers could take tea while watching the films. The cinema was the first to show talking films with Al Jolson in The Singing Fool *in 1929. The Havelock became the Gaumont before its closure and demolition in 1963.*

Vesta Tilley laid the foundation stone of the Empire Theatre which opened in 1907. Although it has shown films it has remained a live theatre. All the great stars of the entertainment world have trodden its boards and it still attracts the best.

The view from the Empire stage showing the grand circle, the upper circle and 'the Gods', The Empire's vast stage lends itself to large-scale productions and extravaganzas. The theatre was designed by a partnership of local architects, Thomas and William Milburn.

Newcastle Road Baths were opened in 1936 and set new standards in convenience and comfort for Wearsiders who were used to the less well-appointed High Street Baths.

Left: The modern interior of Newcastle Road Baths with seating for spectators. At the deep end two springboards and a high board were well used.

Below: Taking coffee in Binns Cafe in the 1930s was a social event in Sunderland. Not only did one sit in fine surroundings but a quartet played music, too. Here, left to right, are: Tommy McDonnell (drums), Ken Cutchie (piano), Bob Gibbon (violin), and Bob Stoker (clarinet and saxophone). This picture was lent by Pat Ayton, Ken Cutchie's daughter.

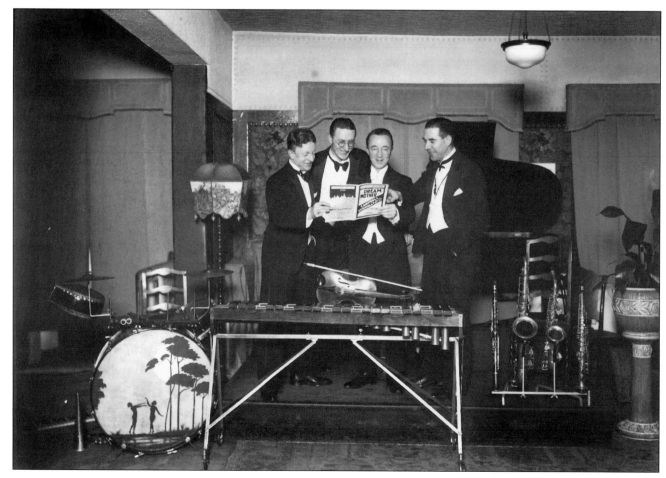

St Gabriel's Church Concert Party 'The Blue Boys' in the 1920s. Bob and Alf Pearson who went on to become household names in the music halls were once members of this troupe. Pat Ayton lent the photograph

A splendid photograph of the Ashbrooke Tennis Tournament of 1905. Note the long dresses worn by the women players and the profusion of floral bonnets among the lady spectators and the straw boaters popular with the men. There is not a pair of shorts in sight.

Fund-raising was the aim of this happy bunch of entertainers in the East End of Sunderland between the wars. They called themselves the Dhobi Wallahs and they wore various pieces of military gear and played all sorts of instruments.

They knew how to hold a street party down in the East End. Here the revellers are celebrating the annual East End Carnival before World War Two.

Workmen are seen putting the finishing touches to grotesque figures that featured in the Roker and Seaburn Illuminations just before the outbreak of war. The figures were part of a tableau illuminated in Roker Park.

Taken in 1952 this photograph shows that the Illuminations were back at Roker and Seaburn brightening up the austerity of post-war Wearside. Tableaux and fountains in the lake made a wonderland for the crowds who came from all over the North-East to see The Lights.

Playtime for children at Southwick Oval before the Second World War. The boys are wrestling and trying to do handstands while the girls, arms linked, appear to be about to start a game. In the background is St Columba's Church.

The happiest days of your life some people say of their schooldays. These children from Simpson Street, School, Sunderland, taken in the 1960s, look as though they have just been given the day off!

Thousands of Wearside schoolchildren will recognise the huts at Seaburn School Camp, where for a week or two they would spend time out in the fresh air or on the beach instead of in their school's classrooms. Who among them will forget, too, the marmalade puddings that used to be served at dinner times?

Usworth Aerodrome was established during World War One but saw real action during World War Two when Hurricanes of 607 County of Durham Squadron RAF fought the German bombers that attacked the North-East. The site is now occupied by the giant Nissan factory.

131

Flags and bunting across the street and doors and windows festooned with flags and streamers meant it was carnival time in the East End. This picture was taken on 26 August, 1930 in Moorgate Street.

A Hawker Hurricane lands back at Usworth during a post-war air day. The Sunderland air days proved so popular that when the Nissan plant took over the site Sunderland Council reintroduced the shows at Roker and Seaburn with enormous success.

Sunderland Air Days were hugely popular. On a fine day, like this one in the 1970s, more than 50,000 people would line the runway to see the supersonic jets and the Red Arrows perform.

An aircraft of the Sir Alan Cobham's Flying Circus pictured at Usworth in the 1930s. The pilot can be seen sitting in the open cockpit at the front of the machine.

There was no greater gathering of merrymakers than the Durham Miners' Gala. After the political speech-making was over it was time for fun and here on the Racecourse they did just that. The crowd in the centre has formed a ring to watch an escapologist who is bound with ropes.

At War

War came to Wearside in 1939 and one of the first tasks for every family was to construct an air-raid shelter. There were indoor ones that resembled a reinforced table. Then there were Morrison shelters, which were solid brick and concrete structures. Most, however, were like this one, an Anderson shelter. Half sunk in the garden it consisted of corrugated metal sheets bolted together and then covered with earth. They saved many a life when the bombs began to fall.

Hitler was even more unpopular on Wearside when his bombers hit Fenwicks Brewery at the bottom of High Street.

Bombed-out. That was the fate of another family at Fulwell early in the war as Wearside suffered at the hands of the bombers that came in the night.

The spectacular Winter Gardens behind Sunderland Museum were shattered by the blast from the bomb that destroyed the nearby Victoria Hall. Sadly the Wearside 'Crystal Palace' was never rebuilt.

Everyone was issued with a gas mask before the war began . . .even little children. Here parents try to reassure a toddler who is being fitted with a gas mask at Commercial Road School in 1939.

A poignant wartime study shows an evacuee leaving Wearside to go to live in the relative safety of the countryside. Many a tearful scene was re-enacted as children carrying knapsacks, gas masks, and with an identity label pinned to their collars, waved goodbye to their parents.

Savings were an important part of the war effort. During Warship Week on Wearside in 1941 a model of the aircraft carrier Ark Royal went on show in Joplings store. It is here being examined by civic leaders including the mayor Myers Wayman.

The women of Wearside took over when the men went to war. Here women set up a lathe for turning operations at a shipyard on the river.

Only the shell of the Binns store at the south-east corner of Fawcett Street remained after German bombers visited the town in April 1941. The damage was caused by incendiary bombs that gutted the building.

Above: Parades through the centre of Sunderland kept up morale during the war. Here a float from Doxfords Shipyard exhibits a girder that would go into a ship to help win the war at sea.

Left: A pitiful scene as a Sunderland man sorts out the few belongings that remain after his home was destroyed in a raid in 1941. Remarkably the mirror in the dressing table to the man's left is intact.

One of the most spectacular events of the war happened in 1940 when a couple of bombs hit the central railway station and blew a carriage out through the roof.

The carriage wheels and part of the station roof ended up in the window of Joseph's sports goods store in Union Street. Here the owner, Mr Monty Joseph, surveys the damage the next day.

PC Jack Hindhaugh stands directing traffic in Park Lane at the Beehive Corner in 1939. The bus is an S.D.O. single-deck on the Ryhope route. The Borough Hotel is still a Vaux house and above street level not a lot has changed in the half century that has passed. The picture has been lent by the policeman's son, Tony Hindhaugh.

A miraculous escape was made by the Martin family of Southwick when their home was bombed in October 1941. The Anderson shelter (arrowed) saved their lives when the bomb exploded.

A distressing task for this Wearside woman. With her home gone she tries to find a few things of value with which to start home-building again.

The lovely old St Thomas's Church in the centre of town fell victim to the bombers in 1943. It was so badly damaged that it was pulled down shortly afterwards.

Even the hallowed turf of Roker Park Football Ground did not escape the bombs. In 1943 a bomb hit the pitch and made this crater.

A parachute mine caused this damage at the Fulwell crossing in 1943. Although umpteen houses were destroyed there were no fatalities, and only eight people were injured.

Tragedy at Pallion. Six people died and nine were injured when German raiders struck in the early hours in April 1941.

The four occupants of this Anderson shelter (foreground) only suffered from shock when a bomb fell nine feet from the shelter partly demolishing houses on either side of them in Huntingdon Gardens, Humbledon, Sunderland.

The Morrison-type shelter (left of picture) saved the lives of a Fulwell man, his wife, and eight-year-old son when his home was destroyed in a raid in 1941.

The German bombers did not have it all their own way, however. Pictured are the wheels of a Heinkel bomber shot down by anti-aircraft fire over Sunderland in 1940. It fell in Suffolk Street and here soldiers examine the undercarriage as the wreckage is cleared away.

Sifting through the wreckage of houses at Monkwearmouth in May 1943 when, in one of the heaviest raids on Wearside, 15 people were killed and 11 injured at this site alone.

Firemen dampen down wreckage at St George's Square, Sunderland, after a parachute mine killed six people and injured 13 in 1943.

In the last raid of the war on Wearside the town received a grievous blow. Twelve people died when the residents' shelter in Lodge Terrace, Sunderland, received a direct hit from a 250-kilo bomb. Ten people were injured.

A group of fire-fighters based at Doxfords Shipyard during the war. The fire engine is a Leyland self-propelled unit and the team fought several big fires on the river and in the docks. The photograph was lent by Mr T.W.Corner.

The war is over and one of the dreaded U-boats that almost brought Britain to its knees during the Battle of the Atlantic is brought into the Wear after the surrender.

VE Day, May 1945 and the terrace at Mowbray Park sees celebratory dancing. Most of the men were not back from the war so many of the girls had to be content to dance with each other.

Fires and Disasters

The greatest fire Sunderland experienced was in 1898. The blaze began in Havelock House and swept through 48 premises around the junction of High Street West and Fawcett Street. In those days Sunderland Fire Brigade was run by the police who had great difficulty organising their hoses because of the crowds which gathered to see the inferno. A certain amount of looting took place even as the fire was being fought.

The Havelock House fire swept across Fawcett Street to burn out Lockhart's Café and surrounding shops. Crowds still came to see the damage days after the event.

Just the shell of Havelock House remains on the site where the Havelock Cinema was eventually to be built. After the fire the town set about improving its fire-fighting services.

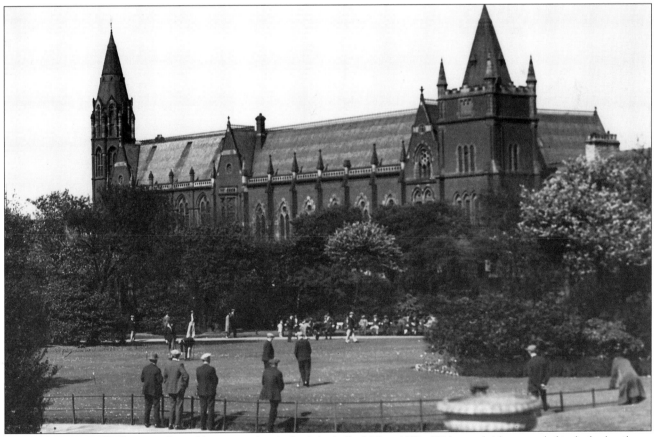

One of the most terrible chapters in theatre history was written in Sunderland. On 16 June 1883, 183 boys and girls were crushed to death when they rushed to claim free toys after a matinee at the Victoria Hall. Some 2,000 children were enjoying the show when it was announced that on leaving each child would receive a present. Immediately there was a rush down the stairs towards the exit. The door was still bolted and the children just piled up on top of each other. The disaster led to the introduction of emergency doors in places of public entertainment.

The memorial to the victims of the Victoria Hall disaster now stands in Bishopwearmouth Cemetery minus its encasement.

Fire-tenders early in the century were still horse powered. Here much to the delight of the small boys watching, a horse-drawn tender goes past the shop of Caslaw, Hayter & Tate which is advertising 50/- suits.

On the evening of 7 November 1962 the Seaham Harbour lifeboat George Elmy was returning to harbour in mountainous seas after picking up four men and a boy from a coble in distress south of the port. Watchers on shore were horrified to see the boat hit by two giant waves as it was about to pass between the piers. It was completely overturned. Eight men and the boy lost their lives. The next day the boat was to be seen overturned on the beach and the whole community of Seaham went into mourning.

The biggest fire of post-war years in Sunderland happened on the night of December 13/14th, 1954, when Joplings department store in High Street West was destroyed in a blaze that could be seen 20 miles away. So fierce was the heat from the fire that glass in premises opposite was shattering with sounds like rifle shots.

Another view of the Joplings fire which completely destroyed the four-floor building. At the time the store was packed with Christmas goods.

Morning brought the sightseers out to view the damage which was estimated at one million pounds. Joplings built their replacement store in nearby John Street.

More than 100 firemen fought the Joplings fire and 20 fire engines from all over the North-East were brought into action.

A spectacular fire occurred at Hardy's furniture store in Fawcett Street in 1972. Seconds before this picture was taken a fireman had rescued three shopworkers down the ladder.

The lovely old St Godric's Church in Durham City had its roof destroyed in a fire in recent years. Here a fireman hoses the roof timbers from an elevated platform. The great tower of Durham Cathedral is seen in the background. The roof of St Godric's was repaired using slates from the recently-closed St Patrick's Church in Sunderland.

Royal Visits

Sunderland has enjoyed many royal visits over the years but none was more appreciated than that made in April, 1943. The town was reeling from heavy bombing raids when King George VI and Queen Elizabeth came to see for themselves the damage wrought by the enemy bombers. The visit was a great morale boost to the folk of Wearside.

The King and Queen toured the shipyards on the Wear and talked to civil defence workers and nurses at a parade in John Street.

Our present Queen was Princess Elizabeth when she came to Sunderland in 1946. She went to Laing's shipyard at Deptford to launch the British Princess on a typically showery April, day.

A smiling Princess Elizabeth mounts the steps to the launch platform before sending the ship down the slipway.

Another task for Princess Elizabeth that day was to open the Eye Infirmary in Queen Alexandra Road. She is pictured here leaving the entrance, which is flanked by nurses, after performing the ceremony.

The Queen and Prince Philip acknowledge the cheers of the Sunderland crowd during their 1954 visit to the town.

Another picture of the new young Queen Elizabeth when she came to Sunderland in 1954 accompanied by Prince Philip who can be seen behind her. Walking with the Queen is the then Mayor of Sunderland, Alderman Mrs J.Huggins.

Its 1977 – Jubilee Year – and the Queen tours Austin & Pickersgill's shipyard where she and Prince Philip were given a rousing reception by the waiting crowd.

Walkabouts had become normal in 1977 and here in Durham City the Queen takes time out to have a chat with some of the crowd.

The Queen and Prince Philip chat to naturalist Peter Scott at the Washington Wildfowl Trust during her Jubilee celebrations.

Girls of the 1st Usworth Guides have a word with Prince Philip during a walkabout at Washington in 1977.

The Jubilee celebrations were a good excuse for people to have a street party. At this one in Pontop Street, East Rainton the children and adults appear to be having the time of their lives.

Sport

A famous painting of the 'The Lads' before they moved to Roker Park in 1898. This is the Newcastle Road ground and a goalmouth scramble is in progress.

Football has always been a passion in the North-East. Practically every works, church, school, and club had its football team. Pictured here before World War Two is the Washington Chemical Works team. Note the trainer with his towel and bag.

In 1937 Sunderland fought their way to the FA Cup Final and this group of supporters is pictured at Sunderland Railway Station before setting off in special trains for Wembley for their game against Preston North End. The picture has been lent by Mrs H.Skelland.

Another group of Wembley-bound supporters pose on the Museum steps before catching their train. The lad (bottom right) has a hat painted with Haway the Lads and Up for the Cup. The photograph has been lent by Mrs Pat Ayton

Above: The team at Wembley on 1
May 1937, was, left to right: back
row: Thompson, Johnston, Gorman,
Mapson, Hall, McNab. Centre:
Cochrane (manager), Carter,
Gurney, Gallacher, Reid (trainer).
Front: Duns and Burbanks. The gate
that marvellous day was 93,495.

The great Bobby Gurney
pictured in action at Wembley.
Sadly Bobby died in early 1994
at the age of 86.

167

After trailing a goal behind at half-time Sunderland equalised six minutes after the restart when Gurney headed in a Burbanks cross. Burns, the Preston North End goalkeeper looks back in despair as the ball hits the back of the net and Gurney turns in triumph. Further goals from Carter and Burbanks gave the Wearsiders a well-deserved victory.

Raich Carter goes up to receive the FA Cup from Queen Elizabeth with King George VI looking on.

Alex Hastings was another Roker favourite who missed the 1937 Cup Final but got his hands on the trophy afterwards. For many years he kept a newsagent's and tobacconist's shop on the seafront beside the Seaburn Hotel before going to live in Australia where he died in 1988.

Raich Carter was a particular favourite of the Roker fans and is seen here in action at the Roker ground before the war.

Many fewer people had cars in the 1950s and match days saw huge crowds crossing Wearmouth Bridge after the game. Gates of 50,000 were commonplace.

The boys' enclosure at Roker Park in the 1960s. Good humour and friendly rivalry was the order of the day. Obscene chants and violence were unknown.

West Southwick School, Sunderland, football team in 1932. Many of these lads would eventually go off to war that came at the end of the decade. Photograph lent by W.Storey.

Cricket was not as popular as football but every schoolboy played it in the summer season. Pictured with a trophy here is the High Southwick School team of 1932. Photograph lent by W.Storey.

Brian Clough was a great favourite with the Roker supporters until serious injury cut short his playing career. A fast and direct centre-forward, he was a thorn in the side of opposition. Wearsiders often ponder what might have been if Clough had stayed on with Sunderland and become the manager.

One of football's greatest entertainers was Len Shackleton. His back-heels and chips were years before their time and his jinking runs with the ball were a delight to see and drew gasps of admiration from the crowds. So great was his pulling power that callers would ring the Echo Office *to find out whether 'Shack' was playing before deciding whether to go to the match at Roker.*

Stan Anderson (left), a strong-tackling right-half and Roker favourite who could also score goals. He and Roker idol Charlie Hurley (right) were the core of the Roker defence for many seasons in the late Fifties and Sixties.

In 1973 the Roker side was back at Wembley with a brilliant team that was to challenge the mighty, all-conquering Leeds United. Bob Stokoe led out 'The Lads' to a tumultuous reception from the many thousands of Wearsiders who made the trip to Wembley. It was to be a memorable day.

"Porterfield" shouted the radio commentator as Ian Porterfield thundered the ball past Leeds goalkeeper Harvey to score the winning goal. The flood of adrenalin and sense of euphoria that swept over Wearsiders at that moment has never been repeated.

The victorious 1973 Sunderland FA Cup winners, left to right, back row: Young (substitute), Halom, Watson, Montgomery, Malone, Pitt. Front row: Horswill, Kerr, Tueart, Hughes, Porterfield and Guthrie.

The Centenary of Sunderland Football Club in 1979 brought several old players together to pose for the cameraman. Left to right, foreground: Billy Bingham, a flying winger; Fred Hall, an old-fashioned stopper centre-half; Jack Stelling, a hard-tackling right-back; George Aitken, a Scottish international half-back; Tommy Reynolds, a tricky left winger with a fierce shot; and Len Shackleton, whose ball skills and entertainment value were without peer.

Above: Wearside had seen nothing like it when the FA Cup was brought home. It took hours for the team to get from the outskirts of town to the Roker ground. Here, with five miles still to go, the crowds cheer The Lads at East Herrington.

The slim figure of international middle-distance runner Brian Hewson who thrilled the Ashbrooke crowds in the mid 1950s with scintillating runs in short-limit handicap mile races. Giving starts of up to 60 yards to good-class runners he would gradually catch and overtake them to snatch victory only in the final straight.

This photograph dates back to the 1880s and it shows Whitburn Cricket club. The cricket caps would raise a smile today but they are worn with great pride in this group.

Ashbrooke Sports Ground in Sunderland was acquired by Sunderland Cricket and Rugby Club in 1887. Since then it has hosted many wonderful sporting events. Australia and several other international touring teams have played cricket there. In post-war years Wimbledon finalists regularly contested the Durham County Open Tennis Tournament on its courts and many of the country's finest athletes and cyclists raced in the annual Police Sports held there. Today, in addition to rugby and cricket, tennis, hockey, squash and bowls clubs are thriving at this attractive ground.

The late, great Colin Milburn made a mark as a schoolboy at Ashbrooke and then went on to greater fame as an England batsman. When he lost an eye in a car accident his career was cut short. Cricket fans still wax lyrical about his big hitting in Test matches.

The attractive Carley Hill cricket ground of Wearmouth Cricket Club is pictured here during a match in the 1970s.

Many a first-class county side would envy the setting of the Durham University ground in the city with its magnificent backdrop of the great Norman Cathedral.

Tom Smith (third from left) was not as well known as Jack 'Cast Iron' Casey (right), the 'Sunderland Assassin', but he was a doughty fighter of yesteryear and upheld the town's fine tradition in the noble art in the mid century.

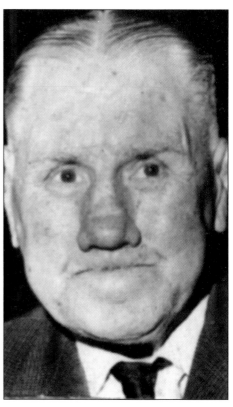

Subscribers

1	Mr Denis Whalen, Mayor of Sunderland	52	Keith Worthy
2	Sir Richard Storey, Bt	53	Mrs J A Suckley
3	Dr Anne Wright	54	Mr W Cox
4	Sir Tom Cowie	55	Anne Greenshields Philpot
5	Sir Paul Nicholson	56	Eileen Kirkaldy
6	C D Brims	57	George Prince
7	S D Bell	58	Dorothy & Arthur Brown
8	P C James	59	Alan Carson
9	A G Hughes	60	R A Waistell
10	K Metcalfe	61	David Watson
11	A Martin	62	Keith Shepherd
12	G Kenny	63	June Bowman
13	G H Toop	64	Mrs Linda A Saville
14	S Gascoigne	65	Robert R Russell
15	M Kearney	66	Mrs Irene Hicks
16	D H Comber	67	Mr Amos Hartis
17	R Warnock	68	James William McCabe
18	M C Boyle	69	Les Robinson
19	Gillian Margret Cook	70	Robert Beckwith
20	Ian Jameson	71	Robert Haswell Wilkinson
21	Marrianne Jane Robson	72	Mrs W Ronald
22	Peter A Barella	73	Norman Taylor
23	Mrs Irene Thompson	74	Kenneth Hardy
24	Sheila Armitage	75	Mr Slassor Walter
25	Doreen Stoker	76	Ernest Longstaffe
26	Paul Batey	77	Pauline Foster
27	Michael J Keirl	78	H D.Parkin
28	Charles Ian Squires	79	Mrs Joyce Goldsmith
29	Joan Pallas	80	M.Pallas
30	Lauren Jobling	81	Dennis Price
31	Pamela C Rodgerson	82	J T Robson
32	Mr J H New	83	T Houghton
33	Linda H Woolston	84	Alan C Finlay
34	R W Hopper	85	Margaret Thornton Lilley
35	William Bell	86	Mrs Margaret McKitterick
36	Mrs V Hudson	87	Mrs Margaret McKitterick
37	John Carrahar	88	A.Thwaites
38	David Sloan	89	J R Elwen
39	Alan Loan	90	Diane Dotchin
40	Alan Howes	91	Arthur Lambton Colquhoun
41	Thomas Sidney	92	George Taylor
42	Eileen Moss	93	John Pallister
43	Mr J Hilton	94	Robet Creighton
44	Thomas Wake	95	Emily Ann Hunter
45	Joseph Leith	96	Brenda Wright
46	Michael Stanley Goodings	97	Frank Sewell Hind
47	Robert Cowe Jnr	98	Ada Douthwaite
48	Ronald Horner	99	Barrett Rodgerson
49	Mr J Tinmouth	100	David Graydon
50	J R Piggett	101	Ernest Graydon
51	James William McRoy	102	Mr D M Fearn

103 Mr & Mrs George Wallace and Mary Rose Spours
104 N I Dugdale
105 Frances Harrison
106 G W Tate
107 Jim D Stokoe
108 Mr & Mrs Thomas Hunter
109 Josephine Frances Watterson
110 Gordon H Fenwick
111 Georgina Hold
112 Mr & Mrs R Brydon
113 Miss Mary Brydon
114 Brenda Dunn
115 Valerie J Holt
116 Kenneth Paul
117 David Hogg
118 J H Dunn
119 Robert Vernon Storey
120 Peter Owen
121 Mrs Janis Moore
122 Jeffrey Park
123 Derek Edward Watts
124 Amelia McQuilliam
125 Hilda F Leith
126 Victoria Helen Baker
127 Amanda Rich
128 W Carney
129 Thomas Barron
130 James Sneddon
131 Mr Gavin Barr
132 Susan Johnson Barkes
133 Gordon Haugh
134 Alfred Bird Rodenby
135 Wilfred Coulson
136 James Thomas Wright
137 Mr William Ray
138 Chrles Robert Morton
139 David Cassap
140 Gordon Sawyer
141 Mrs E C Hartford
142 Mr John Surtees
143 Bill Hern
144 James Patrick Pearson
145 Janet Rooks
146 Pamela Tate
147 Marilyn Campbell
148 E A Watson
149 C J Watson
150 A G Watson
151 Mr David Walker
152 Christopher T G Robson
153 Margaret Holland
154 Henry Edmund Carman
155 Bernard Duncan
156 Mr J H Bulmer
157 Alfred Elstob

158 Eric Bryce
159 Chris Jameson
160 Mr Alan Turley
161 James Richardson
162 Phyllis Jean Wright
163 I D Mills
164 Mr John Richardson
165 Susan Robson
166 Dorothy Oxley
167 Mrs K Cook
168 Ronnie Green
169 Harold Henry
170 Mrs Amber Hunter
171 Mary Atkinson
172 E Smith
173 Edward A Elliott
174 Lawrence Falkner
175 James Orr
176 Edward Nichol
177 Elizabeth Watson
178 Audrey Bones
179 Mr Duncan Scott
180 Peter Mason
181 J E Wynn
182 Norman Hedinburgh
183 Dr H A Davis
184 Ciril Kelso Manson
185 James Mawson Wrightson
186 David T Ferry
187 Yvonne Briggs
188 William Revely
189 R & P French
190 Richard Wilkinson
191 G Cunningham
192 Elizabeth Mitchell
193 Mrs Audrey Maidment
194 Mr George H Brown
195 Stuart George Newton
196 Mr A & Mrs F I Flett
197 Keith Smith
198 Stanley Fowler
199 R Forster
200 Jean Cattermole
201 Clifford Andrew Balbach & Dorothy Anne Balbach
202 Mr Phil Bradford
203 M C Dixon
204 Miss M C Dixon
205 Brenda Mitchinson
206 K Bulmer
207 Margaret Colquhoun
208 Mr Thomas Usher
209 Mr Thomas Usher
210 Mr Harry Holland
211 Mavis Whitfield
212 Mr J Fitzsimmons

213	Mr John Burnell		269	Amy Frost Storey
214	Fred Gooch		270	Joan Quinn
215	Ernest Taylor		271	Howard Percival
216	Alfred Carpenter		272	Frank Deary
217	Valerie West		273	Mrs Hilda Skelland (née Wright)
218	Elizabeth Jane Maughan		274	Mr Charles Ernest Woods
219	Dorothy Bell		275	Norman Trewhitt Potts
220	N S W & K Corner		276	T Gaffney
221	Alan Scott		277	William Mason
222	Robert Derek Lax		278	Mary Veronica Walsh
223	Susan M Bell		279	Mr Robert Wolfendale
224	Mr C B Newby		280	A L de P Woodward
225	Ms Jacqueline Stirling		281	Elizabeth Clark
226	Ms Jacqueline Stirling		282	Mr Peter Dawe
227	Mr John Melvin		283	Mrs Joan McGhin
228	Norman Redman		284	Mrs Gina French
229	David William Jeffrey		285	C J Mann BA Econ, MA, ACA
230	Henry Murray		286	Leslie Storey
231	Mr J Wood		287	Darren Graeme Robson
232	Mrs S A Lewis		288	Mrs Susan Southern
233	Dorothy Hutchinson		289	Mr A Palfeyman
234	Albert Ferguson		290	S & M W Todd
235	Mr B E Little		291	Wm H Ford
236	James Morrell		292	Arthur Roy Taylor
237	Mrs Joan Cockburn		293	William Carruthers
238	Mr David Alcock		294	K T Cummings
239	Mr E Burns		295	Douglas Anderson
240	Robert H Albert		296	Mrs D J Wallace
241	Mr John Teasdale		297	Raymond Hall Davison
242	C E Donkin		298	Derek Anthony Adams
243	Charles Gordon Hodgson		299	E Smith
244	Mrs M Bainbridge		300	E M Mote
245	Mrs M Bainbridge		301	Miss S J Bretherton
246	Joseph Golden		302	John Eggert
247	J Delaney		303	Joyce Starbuck
248	Eric Stephenson		304	Albert Richmond Jones
249	R T Robinson		305	Stephen Johnston
250	Stanley Johnson		306	Edgar Ronald Ambrose
251	David M Caslaw		307	Brian Murray
252	Mr D Trott		308	Mr F S Cook
253	John E Steel		309	Mrs Iris Brettwood
254	Mr A Johnson		310	R W & V Taylor
255	George Malcolm Briggs		311	John Fleming
256	David Loutit		312	George Hudson
257	Frederick Duncan Makin		313	Trevor Johnson
258	James Green		314	W & J H Bell
259	Mr Herbert Rowell		315	Mrs Ruth Stein
260	Carol Foster		316	Mary Curry
261	J W Johnson		317	Anne Donneky
262	Argyle House School		318	Charlton Joseph Innes
263	Mrs D Lawson		319	Alan Alcock
264	M Kilduff		320	Mrs Ellen Powell
265	Mrs B Clyde		321	Mrs Ellen Powell
266	Mr Phillip Lunn White		322	Robert Henry Erskine
267	Dennis R Rodgers		323	Frank Hines
268	Mr H W Taylor		324	Ethel May Sheriff

325	Nora Hope		381	Berwick Hedger
326	Peter Kitts		382	Eric Bailey Smith
327	Lynda Davison		383	Alan Ball
328	Mr R A Finley		384	Veronica Taylor
329	Robert Wild		385	Joan & Bill Laydon
330	Leslie Jones		386	J Stephenson
331	Mr D W Dunthorne		387	Brian Lynn
332	Keith Stout		388	Mr Ronald Wright
333	William Boggon		389	John W Kirtley
334	Mr Robert Henry Bilton		390	David Grice
335	Mr David Scott		391	Mr James William Hutchinson
336	Irene Todd		392	Betty & Ray Wilson
337	Rosemary Pratt		393	George Wright
338	Mrs Pauline Alderson Glendinning		394	Mr & Mrs G W Jenkins
339	Mr & Mrs R Beadle		395	Mr Alan Magnus
340	M B Kirk		396	Ethel H Stewart
341	William Ford		397	Eileen Robertson
342	Charles William Peterson		398	John James Rodgers
343	Irene Palmer Shaw		399	M D Ophield
344	J R Kelly		400	Mr Alan Lax
345	C M Johnson		401	George J Williamson
346	Paul Herring		402	Derek Sowerby
347	Joseph Kenneth Halliday		403	Darren Michael Sowerby
348	Kay Callaghan		404	William Martin
349	D W Garthwaite		405	Mr Ken Graham
350	R E Shotton		406	G D E Wayman
351	Malcolm Gatt		407	Dennis Anthony Potts
352	Henning Lund		408	Gordon Aslett
353	R S Mallam		409	Mr R F Lovegrove
354	John Thomson		410	Marjorie H Marsh (Cuthbertson)
355	J A Whilems		411	R & C S Colling
356	John Benfield Curtis		412	Mr Raymond Allan Jefferson
357	Mr A P Brown		413	Elaine Maxwell Aynsley
358	M Browning		414	Robert and Mildred Green
359	Mr Allan Parkin		415	Albert Render
360	James Potts		416	Elsie Foster Chandler
361	A Donkin		417	Donald Waters
362	Leslie Forth		418	Doris Forster Townes
363	Mark Foley		419	Gordon R Hubbard
364	John Brown		420	John Graydon
365	George Gordon Rutherford		421	Jean McHugh
366	Raymond Hodgson		422	Mavis MacDonald
367	David McGuire		423	Mr Denis Rooney
368	Sydney Halliday		424	Matthew Sidney
369	Dorothy Elizabeth Yendall		425	William Reeve
370	Mary Bowery		426	Alan J Wrightson
371	David Gillespie		427	Robert E Hepple
372	Yvette Murray (née Gair)		428	Irene Dunn
373	Bryan Jones		429	Mrs E M Cassie
374	Elizabeth Greenfield		430	GH Liddle
375	John McClennan		431	J Preston
376	Valerie Willis		432	Mr G Fincham
377	Alan Rollin			
378	T G Cockburn			
379	Robert Crawford			
380	R Rush			